CW01213064

Original title:
Silent Snow, Merry Hearts

Copyright © 2024 Creative Arts Management OÜ
All rights reserved.

Author: Isaac Ravenscroft
ISBN HARDBACK: 978-9916-90-940-9
ISBN PAPERBACK: 978-9916-90-941-6

Elation in the Stillness

In a quiet room, I danced with glee,
Tripped on the rug, oh dear, not me!
The cat gave a glare, paws crossed in disdain,
Wondering why humans can't maintain.

Snowy Sighs

Snowflakes tumble, soft and bright,
Just like my hair on a bad hair night.
Building a snowman, so cold and round,
He melted away before he was crowned.

Heartfelt Smiles

A smile is sweet, like ice cream delight,
But wait, what's that? I've splattered it right!
All over my shirt, now there's a stain,
Guess I'll be stylish in joy and in pain.

Tranquil Twilight

The sky turns pink, a painter's dream,
As fireflies buzz and the crickets scream.
I tripped over grass in a graceful dance,
Wishing I had paid attention at a glance.

Frosty Cheers

With mugs of cocoa, we clink and cheer,
Until someone yells, "Hey, nice sweater, dear!"
Laughter erupts, as marshmallows fly,
Next time perhaps, we'll avoid the pie.

Cherished Whispers in the Frost

In winter's chill, we start to dream,
Snowflakes dance, a frosty team.
Hot cocoa simmers, marshmallows gleam,
We laugh and giggle, what a silly scheme.

Penguins slide on icy ponds,
With lazy waddle, they respond.
Snowmen wearing hats and wands,
They hold secrets of snow-glistened fronds.

Glistening Joys Unfold

Glistening eyes when snowflakes fall,
We build a fortress, oh so tall.
Snowball fights, we giggle and brawl,
Laughter echoes, a winter call.

Ice-cream cones filled with snow,
Not so tasty, but it's a show.
Frosty noses and cheeks aglow,
We trod through frost, with a cheerful 'whoa!'

Hearts Together in the Quiet

In quiet nights with stars so bright,
We share our snacks, what a delight!
Chilly toes wrapped up so tight,
A cozy bubble, pure and right.

Whispers travel through the frost,
With every giggle, we count the cost.
Winter's magic, we never lost,
In our hearts, the laughter's embossed.

Winter's Embrace of Happiness

Winter hugs us with its freeze,
Cozy blankets, oh such ease.
Tickling toes and soft, warm fleece,
In this chill, our joy won't cease.

Hot soup pot bubbling with cheer,
Spicy laughter, winter's dear.
We toast to friends who bring us near,
In frost's embrace, we persevere.

Enchanted Flurries

In the sky they swirl and dance,
Snowflakes twirl, it's a snowy romance.
One landed right upon my nose,
I sneezed, and off it goes!

Snowmen gather, hats askew,
With carrot noses, just for a view.
But while I'm busy giving a wink,
They tip their hats—more snow to drink!

Warmth in the Depths of Winter

Heaters hissing, blankets piled high,
Snug like a bug, oh me, oh my!
But the cocoa's gone, what a plight!
Can I survive this frosty night?

The cat's curled up, a fuzzy ball,
In the warmth of the fridge—wait, that's the wall!
I turn to grab another snack,
But it seems I've lost my mind, oh, hack!

White Shrouds of Happiness

Outside the world's a snowy white,
But here I'm feeling pure delight.
I slip and slide on icy ground,
Who knew winter could be so profound?

Hot soup is bubbling, oh so grand,
While snowflakes land on my upturned hand.
But wages of this winter flair,
Is a snowball fight—beware, beware!

Icicles of Delight

Hanging from roofs, like pointy teeth,
Icicles sparkle, a winter wreath.
I dare not dodge, lest they should fall,
An ice-cold end could spell my all.

But with each drip, laughter fills the air,
As I sip on ice tea without a care.
So here's to winter, our frosty friend,
With chilly giggles that never end!

Merry Whispers

In the corner, there's a cat,
Stealing my holiday hat.
With a wiggle and a grin,
He plots the pounce, let the fun begin!

Cookies vanish, oh so quick,
Was it Santa, or my dog named Rick?
The lights blink in a merry dance,
As I trip on tinsel, oh what a chance!

Festive Flurries

Snowflakes fall, but so do pies,
Here comes grandma, oh what a surprise!
With a wink and a smile, she'll bake all day,
At the door, the dog cheers, 'Hooray, hooray!'

Eggnog spills with a fluffing cheer,
The tree sways—it's that time of year!
A partridge in an old pine tree,
Wondering where its breakfast could be.

Delicate Dreams

In the night, I've lost my sock,
Underneath the ticking clock.
Elves are giggling, full of cheer,
Plotting mischief, they draw near!

Hot chocolate spills on my brand-new shirt,
Santa laughs, 'Oh, what a flirt!'
The marshmallows dance, oh what a sight,
Wishing I had extra delight.

Warm Hues in the Chill

Bundled up in Grandad's coat,
I wobble like a big old goat.
Snowmen chuckle, well, they try,
With spare carrots and a winked eye.

My mittens mismatched, a fashion no-no,
While singing carols off-key fast and slow.
The world's aglow with laughter bright,
Warm hues twinkling in the night.

Softly Falling Love

In a world of clumsy grace,
I tripped on love's embrace.
With cookies in my hand,
I won your heart, oh so grand.

Like snowflakes on a cake,
You thought I was a mistake.
But as we laughed and played,
Our goofy love was made.

Chill of Bliss

Sipping cocoa, feeling grand,
In mittens, we hold hands.
A snowman in your hat,
Oh no! He's gone splat!

We dance in frosty air,
With snowflakes in our hair.
Our giggles fill the night,
As penguins join our flight.

Evenings of Crystal Softness

The moon is made of cream,
We laugh and share a dream.
In jackets stuffed with fluff,
Tonight, we've got enough.

Marshmallows float in tea,
You said, "Look, that's a bee!"
We turned to see its flight,
And accidentally took a bite.

Echoes of Frost

The wind whispers a tune,
As we chase a dancing moon.
With ice skates on our feet,
We twirled in funny feats.

But then you did a flip,
And landed on your hip.
With laughter ringing clear,
We stayed, my dear, right here.

Heartfelt Choreography

In the kitchen, I try to dance,
But I trip on my cat's little prance.
Spinning around with flour in the air,
My dog's breaks it up with a confused stare.

My partner jumps in, thinks it's a game,
But on the floor, there's a slippery stain.
We twirl and we stumble, quite the sight,
A living room waltz, what a clumsy delight!

The vacuum cleaner joins with a roar,
As we dodge it again, oh, what a chore!
We laugh at the mess on the lovely floor,
In this heartfelt dance, who could ask for more?

So grab your broom, let's shift the mood,
We'll tango with dust while singing a tune.
With a heart full of laughter, we'll glide with flair,
In our kitchen ballet with snacks everywhere!

Twinkling Footprints

Little feet dashing on the soft grass,
Making twinkling patterns that quickly pass.
With each tiny step, a giggle escapes,
As they chase after butterflies, magical shapes.

Sandy toes leaving trails, oh what fun,
Building castles in the sunshine, second to none.
With fingers in the frosting, they make a mess,
Chocolate-covered cheeks, oh what a success!

Raindrops start falling, what a grand race,
Splashing in puddles, their joyful embrace.
Tiny footprints leading down to the creek,
In their rubber boots, they dance and squeak.

As night falls, stars twinkle, a sight so sweet,
Little voices hum lullabies, soft and neat.
In every footprint, a memory shines,
Of playful adventures, in simple designs.

Celestial Snowfall

Flakes like feathers dance in the air,
Covering streets with a soft, fluffy layer.
Kids rush outside with their mittens on tight,
Crafting snowmen with noses, a carrot delight!

Snowball fights starting, laughter so loud,
Making the neighbors peek out, so proud.
With hats on our heads and boots so tall,
We build a snow fort, ready for a brawl!

But on our way in, we slip and we slide,
Hot cocoa awaits, it's a slippery ride.
We giggle and shiver, cheeks rosy and bright,
Warming up inside from our chilly delight.

So let the snowfall keep coming, we'll play,
With rosy cheeks and smiles to brighten our day.
In this winter wonderland, we frolic and cheer,
Creating memories, our hearts full of cheer.

Winter's Gentle Caress

Snowflakes dance with glee,
As I trip on my shoe.
I swear they laugh at me,
This winter's quite the zoo.

Icicles drip like a tease,
Forming daggers on the eaves.
With every breath, I freeze,
Winter's got tricks up its sleeves.

My nose is red as a beet,
Hot cocoa rules the day.
But in snow, I use my feet,
To slip and slide away!

Sledding down with style,
I scream and yell with cheer.
Then crash, I'm in a pile,
Winter, you bring me near!

Hearts Unfolding

Two hearts start to flutter,
Like butterflies in spring.
But wait, what's that? Oh butter!
It's toast, my favorite thing.

I wrote you a love note,
It's stuck on my pet's fur.
It flew away like a boat,
But that's love, I infer!

We met at the coffee shop,
You spilled on my new shirt.
I laughed until I plop,
You smiled, saying, "O dirt!"

Hearts open wide and true,
With laughter as our plan.
In love, we'll stick like glue,
When you trip, I'll be your fan!

Snow-Blanketed Fantasies

In the winter wonderland,
Where snowmen come to life,
I lost my mitten, oh man!
This snowy day's a strife.

My dreams are made of cheese,
With snowflakes lickin' toes.
I build a fort with ease,
While my hands are turning froze.

Snowball fights, oh what a blast,
Until I slip and fall.
Laughter echoes, what a cast,
We'll laugh and have a ball!

At twilight's soft embrace,
Our footprints mark the way.
Winter's magic, such a grace,
In dreams, we want to stay!

Laughter in the Drift

Amid the fluffy snow,
I saw a puppy play.
He dove in with a flow,
And made my heart say "yay!"

With snowflakes on my nose,
I roll and tumble down.
The cold wind gently blows,
Yet I wear a happy frown.

Kids build forts and capes,
While adults just complain.
In snow, we change our shapes,
Like penguins on a train!

But laughter fills the air,
And joy melts every chill.
In winter's gentle care,
Our hearts find warmth and thrill!

The Quietude of Twinkling Frost

Frosty flakes dance on nose,
Like tiny elves in winter's clothes.
The quietude is quite a sight,
Unless you slip—a snowy fright!

Hot cocoa's call, so warm and sweet,
While snowmen plan a sneaky feat.
They'll roll away with all their might,
Just watch your back—hold on tight!

Blankets snug, oh what a treat,
Trapped indoors, we can't be beat!
We sing to cheer, though voices croak,
In a snowball fight, we're just a joke!

With twinkling stars that wink with glee,
The frosty air shouts, "Come play with me!"
As winter whispers soft and low,
Laughter echoes through the snow.

Cuddled in Dreamy Flurries

Flurries swirl, a soft embrace,
Cozy corner, perfect place.
With fuzzy socks and cheesy snacks,
Hiding from the chilly whacks!

Dreams of penguins on parade,
Dancing 'round in winter's shade.
They'll waddle in from cold outside,
While we all snuggle, eyes open wide!

The cat's an expert on the couch,
In winter's lap, he's quite the slouch.
He dreams of fish, fresh from the sea,
While we sip tea, blissfully!

Snowmen pop up, faces bright,
In hats and scarves, what a sight!
Yet, when they melt, oh what a shame,
Water puddles? Who's to blame?

Mirth Beneath the Falling Sky

Snowflakes giggle as they fall,
Tickling noses, having a ball.
Each fluffy touch a playful tease,
Laughter hides amidst the freeze!

In winter wonder, joy abounds,
With silly songs and jolly sounds.
The snow grows tall, we shout and play,
Until we trip—what a display!

Hot ice cream? It's a winter treat,
Oh dear! The flavors can't be beat.
But slippery roads lead to surprise,
Watch where you step—it's a wild ride!

As clouds hang low and winter sighs,
Underneath, a million spies.
Each flake of joy falls with delight,
Mirth abounds in frosty white!

Love in the Lap of Winter

Wrapped in warmth—the perfect date,
Sipping cocoa, feel the fate.
Gazing into eyes so bright,
Love's a snowstorm, pure delight!

Fingerless gloves, a chilly plight,
But hand in hand, it feels just right.
With every slip upon the ice,
We laugh it off; oh, isn't love nice?

Snowball fights become a game,
As you call me by my name.
With cheeky grins and frosty breath,
Our joy is stronger than winter's death!

In every flake, a tiny heart,
We'll craft our dreams, a joyful art.
For in this season, love will shine,
In winter's lap, you're always mine!

Enchanted by Winter's Tenderness

Snowflakes dance like tiny stars,
Softly landing near my car.
A winter chill has kissed my nose,
I tripped on ice and struck a pose.

Penguins in their tuxedos glide,
While squirrels in their coats take pride.
I build a snowman, tall and round,
He stares at me, then falls down!

I sip on cocoa, oh so sweet,
Marshmallows float like fluffy fleet.
My fingers numb, I cannot type,
But I'm too happy, who needs the hype?

In mittens thick, I wave goodbye,
To winter's charm, oh how I sigh.
But spring will come with little doubt,
And take my snowmen out, no clout!

Glimmers of Cheer Amidst the Frost.

Frosty windows, such a sight,
I see my breath in morning light.
The dog is barking at a bird,
He leaps and lands, oh how absurd!

Icicles hang like crystal teeth,
My lips are chapped, oh what a grief!
Hot soup is slurped with great delight,
While snowballs fly, oh what a fight!

Sledding down the hill, I scream,
My face is cold, I start to dream.
Building forts with friends galore,
But someone's stuck, can't take it anymore!

Yet as the days go slowly by,
A sunny ray will catch my eye.
With snowmen gone, we'll dance and cheer,
Until next winter, we hold dear!

Whispers of White

Winter whispers with a grin,
A snowball fight is sure to win.
I dodge and weave, I laugh and shout,
But someone got me, now I'm out!

The frozen pond, a skating spree,
I twirl and spin, what's wrong with me?
A slip, a fall, I cannot stand,
The ice now rules this slippery land!

Hot cider warms my chilly hands,
While snowflakes fall in frosty bands.
The world is white, a giant quilt,
But who will help me when I wilt?

Yet in this chill, there's joy to find,
With friends and fun, we're all aligned.
The whispers soft, the laughter bright,
We'll treasure this enchanted night!

Frosted Dreams

In dreams of snow, I skip and play,
I build a palace, hip-hip-hooray!
The frosty air is crisp and clear,
My snow dog barks, "Come play right here!"

Under the stars, we laugh and glide,
On making snow angels, we take pride.
But who's that frowning? Oh dear me,
It's just my neighbor, behind a tree!

Fingers numb from snowball thrills,
My cheeks are flushed, I've got the chills.
But as I sip my chocolate treat,
I feel the warmth from head to feet!

So here's to winter, frosty and bright,
With laughter shared, it feels so right.
Let's frolic on till spring is here,
In frosted dreams, we'll shed our fear!

Gentle Flakes

Snowflakes dance with grace,
Like little stars in space.
They land upon my nose,
And tickle me, I suppose.

They swirl and twist in air,
A winter waltz, so rare.
I catch them on my tongue,
A frosty treat, so young.

They blanket all the ground,
In silence, joy is found.
Each flake a whimsy small,
Together, they enthrall.

With mittens on my hands,
I build my snowman plans.
He grins with coal for eyes,
In winter mischief, we rise.

Warm Embrace

The heat of coffee brews,
As winter bids adieu.
I hug my mug so tight,
Like a friend on a cold night.

With blankets piled high,
In my chair, I comply.
I sip and taste the bliss,
Each warm hug, I won't miss.

The fire crackles bright,
Its glow feels just right.
My slippers hug my feet,
Winter can't be beat!

As snowflakes fall outside,
I cozy up with pride.
With snacks and all the cheer,
I embrace winter here.

Winter's Warm Beneath the Stars

Beneath the frosty night,
The stars twinkle so bright.
I sip on cocoa sweet,
While bundled from my feet.

The snowflakes softly land,
Like whispers from the land.
They glitter in moonlight,
A dreamscape of delight.

With friends, we laugh and sing,
Wrapped tightly in this thing.
We share marshmallows toasted,
In winter, hearts are coasted.

So, grab another chair,
Let laughter fill the air.
Together, we all gleam,
In winter's lovely dream.

Shiver of Joy

The cold wind gives a shiver,
But joy is what I deliver.
In boots that squeak and slide,
I conquer winter with pride.

Snowmen with blushy cheeks,
They giggle as winter peaks.
The sledding hill awaits,
For playful, snowy mates.

With rosy cheeks aglow,
We frolic in nature's show.
Hot cocoa, the great prize,
To warm up frozen ties.

So let the cold winds blow,
Our spirits always glow.
A shiver, what a joy,
As winter's sleek decoy.

Hushed Wonders

In winter's hush, I've found,
A world of joy profound.
The snowflakes softly fall,
In beauty, they enthrall.

Footprints mark the quiet,
A moment so sublime yet.
I tiptoe through the white,
In nature's calm invite.

The trees wear coats of frost,
As I ponder what is lost.
But in this still embrace,
I see the magic's face.

So here I stand and stare,
At wonders everywhere.
In winter's quiet song,
I know that I belong.

Laughter Wrapped in Flurries

Snowballs fly, oh what a sight,
Frosty faces, smiles so bright.
We slip and slide, a comical dance,
In winter's grip, we take a chance.

Hot cocoa spills, what's the fuss?
Laughter echoes, all of us.
A snowman's hat falls to the ground,
And giggles linger all around.

Frost-Kissed Grins

Children giggle, what a thrill,
Rolling in snow, oh what a chill!
With noses red from winter's bite,
They build their dreams in pure delight.

Sleds go flying, hearts collide,
As parents watch with smiles wide.
Frost-kissed grins and rosy cheeks,
These are the joys that winter speaks.

Chilling Peace

The world is quiet, snowflakes land,
A perfect scene, so softly planned.
With every flake, a hush divine,
Nature's quilt, all intertwined.

Yet in this calm, there's laughter still,
A snowman's grin, a wind's sweet thrill.
Chilling peace wrapped in cozy cheer,
Winter's whispers, oh so clear.

Cozy Joy

Fireplaces crackle, popcorn pops,
In fuzzy socks, our laughter hops.
Pillows piled, a fortress grand,
Hot chocolate calls with a sippy hand.

Out the window, snowflakes play,
While we bask in warmth, hooray hooray!
Cozy joy fills the air we breathe,
In simple moments, we believe.

Glimmering Silence

In a world of white, silence reigns,
But warmth of laughter breaks the chains.
Even as stars above twinkle bright,
Our silly antics light up the night.

With snowmen grinning, hats askew,
A playful snow fight, who knew?
Glimmering silence holds the fun,
As winter's magic has just begun.

Warmth in the Chill

When winter's breath is icy and bold,
We gather 'round, stories told.
With hot cocoa in a mug so snug,
We're warm inside, like a joyful hug.

The snowflakes dance, the wind gives chase,
Yet here we are, in our cozy space.
We wear our socks, mismatched and bright,
And laugh at the cold, with all of our might.

Outside we shiver, bundled and tight,
While inside we giggle, what a sight!
The chill may bite, but hearts do thrill,
In our little haven, against the chill.

So raise a toast, to winter's embrace,
With shared warm tales, we find our place.
As we sip and thaw, what a delightful spill,
Our spirits soar, we conquer the chill.

Echoes of a Winter's Joy

The snowflakes whisper in frosty air,
Each flake a giggle, a playful dare.
We roll in the drifts, come snow or sleet,
In winter's embrace, we can't be beat.

Hot soup is served, it's quite a feast,
With bread so warm, we munch, at least.
Outside the cold, but inside we sway,
To the echoes of laughter, come join the play.

Sledding down hills, we fly and scream,
Each winter moment, a silly dream.
With frigid noses and cheeks that glow,
We're kings and queens of the winter show.

So gather your friends, don't let them flee,
Let's dance with the snow, oh what glee!
For in every flake, let joy deploy,
This is the beauty, of winter's joy.

Hushed Dance of Snowflakes

Beneath the streetlamp's soft, warm glow,
Snowflakes twirl in a silent show.
They swirl and dip, they don't complain,
Winter's dancers, falling like rain.

Each one unique, a frosty surprise,
They land on noses, on chins and eyes.
A gentle ballet, no music to hear,
Just the soft whispers of winter cheer.

We catch them with tongues, and giggles abound,
As we chase the flakes that fall to the ground.
A hush in the air, as if time stands still,
In this winter waltz, all hearts we fill.

So waddle like penguins, and slide on the ice,
Each step's a laugh, oh, isn't it nice?
With laughter and joy, not a care it takes,
In this hushed dance of delightful snowflakes.

Hearts Alight in Stillness

The world turns white, a still tableau,
As winter wraps all in a cozy glow.
With fires blazing, we snuggle tight,
Hearts alight in the peaceful night.

Outside the frost, but inside we play,
With games and laughter, we brighten our day.
A blanket fort, our fortress of dreams,
In our warm enclave, joy beams and gleams.

So toast to the season, let spirits rise,
With friend's silly faces, and surprise pies.
In jovial whispers, and moments we steal,
Hearts alight, winter's warmth is real.

So cherish the stillness, the quiet and calm,
With mugs of delight, and winter's sweet charm.
Let's gather the warmth in this frosty thrill,
Our hearts warmed together, a magical chill.

Love in a Winter Wrap

In winter coats, we snuggle tight,
Like two warm burritos, what a sight!
Hot cocoa spills, oh what a mess,
But in your arms, I must confess.

The snowflakes fall, a frosty dance,
We trip and laugh, it's true romance!
Your nose is red, my cheeks a glow,
Together in cold, our love will grow.

We build a snowman, not a clue,
With a stick for arms, he'll dance with you!
Yet he tips over, laughs he brings,
We roll around like silly things.

So here we sit, in winter's grasp,
My mug in hand, your fingers clasp.
We'll cozy up, the night is young,
In winter's wrap, our hearts are sung.

Cheers Amidst the Quiet

The world is hush, the night is still,
Yet in my heart, there's a warm thrill.
With cocoa mugs, we clink and cheer,
To silly dreams that bring us near.

Snowflakes twirl like dancers, grand,
We make a toast, hand-in-hand.
To snowball fights and heated pranks,
In tranquil nights, let's fill the tanks!

The quiet hum of winter air,
With giggles shared, we light the flair.
We sip our drinks, with straws like fish,
Fulfilling every winter wish.

So here's to love in frosty zones,
Where giggles echo, and joy condones.
With every sip, let laughter flow,
Cheers to the quiet, let it glow!

Elysium of White

In a land where snowflakes softly land,
We dance around, hand in hand.
The world is white, a frosty scene,
In this elysium, we reign as queen.

Sledding down the slopes so steep,
In giggles and shouts, joy takes a leap.
With cheeks like cherries, we race and glide,
In this winter wonder, we take pride.

Snow angels made beneath the pine,
With laughter echoing, divine!
Each flake a peanut, on our skin,
And in this bliss, we twirl and spin.

So raise a glass, let's take a flight,
In our paradise of pure delight.
With every flurry, our hearts will sing,
In this elysium, joy we bring.

Dances in the Frost

In the glow of winter's light,
We dance around, what a sight!
With feet like ice, we slide away,
In clumsy moves, we laugh and sway.

The frosty air is crisp and cold,
Yet with your warmth, I feel bold.
Spin me 'round, let's not get lost,
In this joyous, frosty frost.

We slide and stumble, grace amiss,
Each fall we take is pure bliss.
Snowflakes falling soft and sweet,
Together we make our own beat.

So let's embrace this frosty art,
With giggles shared, you warm my heart.
In winter's dance, with joy we find,
A laughter shared, our hearts entwined.

Frosty Musings

When snowflakes land upon my nose,
I wonder how a snowman grows.
With carrots snoozing in the yard,
He dreams of winter, oh so hard.

With scarves wrapped round and mittens tight,
I slip and slide, what a delight!
The icicles dangle like toothy grins,
As winter laughs, and chaos begins.

The dog in snow, a furry ghost,
Chasing his tail, he loves it most.
We giggle as he leaps and bounds,
Creating snow-dogs all around.

And as the sun sets on this game,
The stars appear, but oh, the shame!
For once the snow starts turning brown,
We'll have to pack the fun right down.

Joyful Reflections

Hot cocoa with marshmallows so sweet,
Brings joy that cannot be beat.
I sip and sigh, it warms my soul,
While visions of chocolate start to roll.

The cat doing backflips, oh what a sight,
Chasing her tail, she's full of fright.
With each jump, she knocks down a glass,
While I just sit, hoping she'll pass.

A snowman's hat blown off by the breeze,
Causing giggles as I sneeze.
The neighbors call to share a cheer,
As we all gather, winter's near.

Then comes the night, with stars aglow,
We sing of joy, and let it flow.
With friends around, we laugh and play,
Making merry in every way.

Melodies in the Winter Air

Jingle bells ringing, what a delight,
As snowflakes twirl, oh what a sight.
I whistle tunes as I stomp through snow,
Creating music wherever I go.

The squirrel's dance on a slippery branch,
Trying his luck with a frosty chance.
A winter waltz, just him and me,
As we shimmy through the frost so free.

With snowball fights that never cease,
We toss and duck, oh what a piece!
Laughter echoes through the trees,
While everyone falls with merry sneezes.

As day turns to night, the stars align,
Hot cocoa bubbles, oh so divine.
We raise our mugs to winter's flair,
Sipping tunes in the frosty air.

Frost-Edged Smiles

With frosty breath, I step outside,
To join the world in winter's ride.
The trees wear coats of glistening white,
While I make snow angels, quite a sight!

The little kids run wild with glee,
Tumbling down hills, so carefree.
They build their forts, oh what a show,
While I stand back, chuckling low.

The snowflakes dance, all shiny and bright,
Each one unique, a frosty light.
They tickle my nose, and I cannot resist,
To taste the joy that winter insists.

As evenings fall and candles glow,
We swap our tales of the winter woe.
With every chuckle, every thread,
Frost-edged smiles paint joy instead.

Whispers of Winter's Embrace

Snowflakes fall with gentle grace,
Turning cheeks to rosy lace.
Froze my toes and lost a glove,
Winter's chill, not what I love.

Sipping cocoa by the fire,
Dreaming of a sun's desire.
Though my nose is pink and keen,
I hit the slopes—a snowy scene!

Slipping, sliding, down I go,
Spraying snow—oh, what a show!
Laughter echoes, spirits soar,
Till I land right on the floor!

So here's to winter, crisp and bright,
With frosty mornings, pure delight.
But when the spring blooms, take my hand,
We'll dance on grass, and that's the plan!

Frosted Dreams Beneath a Canopy

Underneath the frosted trees,
Sipping tea, oh, what a tease!
Beneath a blanket, warm and tight,
We dream of summer's golden light.

But who can shift this snow with ease?
It clings to socks, it's in my keys!
Mittens tangled, laughter bursts,
At winter games, our humor thirsts.

Snowmen smile with carrot nose,
But wait! That's just a pose, I suppose.
With their buttons all askew,
I guess they're dressed just like me too!

So let the snowflakes swirl and twirl,
In winter's arms, our joy unfurl.
We'll laugh and dance in chilly bliss,
Till spring arrives and gives a kiss!

Laughter Wrapped in White

Wrapped in layers, snug and warm,
We venture out, away from harm.
But hold on tight to that hot drink,
Or it'll spill—oh, don't you think?

Snowballs flying, aiming high,
I duck and dodge, oh me, oh my!
But when I slip and take a dive,
The laughter echoes, I feel alive!

Frosted windows tell the tale,
Of cozy nights and epic fail.
With games of charades and pies galore,
Who knew winter was quite the chore?

But when the sun melts it away,
We'll cherish those snowy play days.
Till next winter's icy grasp appears,
We'll hold onto the fun through the years!

Nightfall's Gentle Blanket

As night descends, stars start to peek,
The world transforms, so calm, so sleek.
With snowflakes twirling, a soft embrace,
Winter's magic, a dreamy place.

Wrapped in layers, I brave the chill,
Building snow forts, what a thrill!
Hot chocolate spills, and laughter loud,
In this frozen wonderland, I'm proud.

Whispers of snowflakes swirl in the air,
Every breath steals a moment rare.
Warming our hearts with every giggle,
As snowmen dance, and children wiggle.

So as night falls, let's raise a cup,
To winter's charm that lifts us up.
With laughter wrapped in a fluffy mound,
Joy in our hearts, where love is found!

Joyful Crystals

In a land where crystals dance,
They jiggle and they prance.
With sparkles all around,
They mimic every sound.

A crystal ball on a spree,
Whispers secrets playfully.
It tells of socks that shouldn't match,
And snacks that are the perfect catch.

Jubilant gems with cheeky glee,
Plan a party for you and me.
They'll play games of hopscotch too,
Inviting every shade and hue.

So gather round, don't miss the fun,
With joyful crystals, everyone!
A giggle or two, some jokes to share,
In the magical light of crystal flare.

Hibernal Embrace

Winter comes with a warm hug,
Like a bear with a coffee mug.
He snoozes through the snowy days,
Dreaming of hot chocolate bays.

Snowflakes dance like little sprites,
Frosty noses, cozy nights.
With blankets piled high and tight,
We snuggle in, what a sight!

The cold can't chase away the cheer,
Hot cocoa waiting, never fear!
Laughter echoes through the frost,
In hibernal hugs, we never lost.

So sip your drink, enjoy the freeze,
While winter whispers with such ease.
Embrace the chill, it's not too late,
For cuddles with friends are always great!

Chilly Heartbeats

When winter wraps us in its cold,
Heartbeats thump, both brave and bold.
They click like ice on frozen lakes,
Creating rhythms, for goodness' sakes!

Hot soup's the heart's delight,
A steamy bowl in frosty night.
With every spoon, a giggle grows,
'Til laughter spills, and the warmth flows.

Woolly socks on every toe,
Dancing like there's nowhere to go.
With chilly heartbeats, we groove and sway,
Loving winter in the weirdest way!

So grab your mittens, let's take a chance,
We'll frolic through this winter dance.
With every heartbeat, sweet and clear,
We'll cherish the cold, year after year!

Trending Nights of Peace

In a world where trends are crazy,
Nights of peace seem quite hazy.
But find a spot beneath the stars,
Where silence hums and no one spars.

With stars on TikTok floating by,
They spark our dreams to dance and fly.
In cozy wraps, we share our thoughts,
In trending nights, peace is what we sought.

So put away your phones for now,
Let's take a moment, take a bow.
With laughter echoing far and near,
We'll toast to peace with a loud cheer!

So gather close, let worries cease,
In trending nights, we find our peace.
A viral smile can last all night,
As we drift softly into twilight.

Glistening Delights

Ice cream in the winter night,
Melting fast, what a fright!
Snowmen taste the chilly spree,
But they're just ice, not for me.

Cookies shine on snowy trees,
Charmed by frost, they laugh with ease.
Hot cocoa spills, has quite a flair,
Stains my shirt, but I don't care!

Candied apples, sticky sweet,
Slipping down a frosty street.
Snowball fights, we laugh out loud,
Except when we hit mom, she's proud!

Marshmallows float, like fluffy dreams,
A snow globe bursting at the seams.
With every bite, we find delight,
Winter's here, what a silly sight!

Hearts Aglow

Cupid's arrow takes a leap,
Straight into my friend's old jeep.
Love notes hidden, poorly penned,
But they'll get moonlight in the end.

Valentines made from old coupons,
Promised hugs and silly brawns.
Chocolates shaped like old dog bones,
What a gift for those who moan!

Dancing hearts, we twirl around,
Laughter's echo fills the ground.
Lovers giggle, feel the spark,
Until they trip and fall in dark!

Dinner dates with awkward cheers,
Spaghetti can lead to great fears.
Slurping noodles, what a show,
But everyone's heart's aglow!

Snowflakes and Sweet Whispers

Snowflakes twirl like little spies,
Whispering secrets as they rise.
Frosty jokes in frozen air,
Who knew winter loved to share?

Flurry of flakes, a dazzling dance,
Laughter echoes with each chance.
Snowmen giggle, hats askew,
Where's their carrot? Have they blew?

Sugar plums in frosty beams,
Chasing winter's icy dreams.
Sipping soup, we tell our tales,
While kittens chase their snowy trails.

Mittens lost in the snowy drifts,
Each one hoping for some gifts.
But snowflakes giggle, swirl and play,
Sweet whispers melt the cold away!

Moments of Frosty Solitude

Standing still in frost's embrace,
Snowflakes dance in soft, white lace.
A moment lost, just me and me,
Hoping winter sets me free.

Penguin waddles on the ice,
Tipping over, oh, that's nice!
Thought I'd join him, oh so bold,
Then I slipped, and stories told!

Sipping tea by fire's glow,
Watching snowflakes plot their show.
Cuddled tight in woolly seams,
Winter's chill fuels all my dreams.

But solitude has quirks galore,
It's just me, and the fridge door.
More snacks please, in frosty awe,
With every bite, I find my flaw!

Enchanted Nights in Icy Hues

The moonlight slipped on icy shoes,
Dancing with owls, sharing their views.
A snowman tried to do the cha-cha,
But fell on his nose and yelled, "Ha ha!"

Frosty fairies, giggling with glee,
Chasing their tails, oh, just wait and see.
They painted houses with shimmering light,
While the neighbors all wondered what went right.

Sipping cocoa with marshmallows afloat,
I toasted a muffin, forgot it, oaf!
A penguin strolled by, tipped his beak,
Said, "Nice dance moves, but your timing's weak!"

In this enchanted night so grand,
All snowflakes conspire, make jubilant plans.
With frosty treats made from goofy delight,
Who knew winter could be such a night?

Radiance of the Frosty Dawn

The sun peeked in with a frosty grin,
Painting the world with a chilly kin.
Hot cocoa brewed in a gingerbread pot,
What would we do without winter's plot?

Snowflakes twinkled, like diamonds on trees,
A squirrel was stuck, begging for cheese.
Between gigs, he posed with a confident flair,
Said, "Watch me slide, it's a known circus affair!"

Rugged mittens, mismatched, what a sight!
Each thumb a compass, pointing to fright.
Yet laughter echoes through snowy hills,
As we tumble about, bursting with thrills.

So here's to dawn, all frosty and bright,
With giggles and wiggles, pure snowy delight.
Let's make silly snow angels and cheer,
For winter's a show, and the stars are near!

Joyful Secrets in the Snowfall

Snowflakes whispered secrets so sweet,
In the woods, doing silly tricks on their feet.
A rabbit declared, "Let's have a ball!"
While tripping over snow, oh what a fall!

Nutty squirrels with acorns galore,
Said, "We'll play twister, then nap on the floor!"
With flipping and flopping, we all took turns,
Creating a chaos that brightly burns.

Penguins practiced their finest ballet,
While deer giggled at the frosty display.
We danced in the snowfall, hearts full of cheer,
Making memories as the winter drew near.

So here's to secrets and laughter so grand,
In the chilly air, let's all take a stand.
For joyful moments, with winter's sweet call,
Are the best types of treasures in the magical fall!

Under the Glittering Veil

Beneath a twinkle of stars on high,
Frogs in tuxedos croaked an opera nigh.
With snowflakes tumbling, oh what a show,
They slipped and slid, creating a glow!

A bunny in boots passed by with a wink,
Said, "Save some snow for a cool icy drink!"
As icicles wobbled, they wouldn't behave,
Shouting, "Make room, we've a party to pave!"

The owls hooted tunes, their owlish cheer,
While snowmen joined in, feeling quite dear.
With carrots for noses and laughter to spare,
They boogied and hopped without any care.

So under this veil, so glittery bright,
Let's gather together and dance through the night.
With joy and confetti made of pure snow,
We'll celebrate winter, let the good times flow!

Joy in the Stillness

In the quiet, I find my snack,
A cookie or two, I won't hold back.
The stillness hums a joyful tune,
Between each bite, I might just swoon.

A nap's a joy that's hard to beat,
Especially when you're off your feet.
With blankets piled up to the chin,
I dream of pizza, oh where to begin!

The world outside may spin and whirl,
But in my mind, I've got a pearl.
A treasure chest of funny thoughts,
In stillness, laughter stirs the pots.

So let's embrace this lovely pause,
With goofy jokes and silly laws.
For joy is found in quiet places,
Where laughter dances, and joy embraces.

Frosted Magic

Winter's here, the snowflakes dance,
Creating magic with every chance.
I step outside in boots so grand,
And promptly slip, oh what a stand!

The trees are dressed in crystal white,
While I look like a frosted fright.
My nose it seems has found a freeze,
Still, I stomp around like a sneeze.

A snowman grins with carrot charm,
I wish to join, but lose my arm.
His smile's bright, my face a mess,
We share a laugh, oh what a guess!

So here we twirl in winter's show,
A frosted scene, a snowy glow.
For laughter thrives where cold winds blow,
In frosted magic, joy will flow.

Shimmering Chill

The air is crisp, my breath's a cloud,
In this dim light, I laugh out loud.
With layers piled and boots so thick,
I waddle like a frozen stick.

Each step I take makes crunching sounds,
I'm a winter's knight, battlegrounds.
With snowflakes falling in my hair,
I am a sight, beyond compare!

The shimmer of ice upon the ground,
A disco floor, my moves are found.
I slip and slide, a comedic show,
As icicles dangle, with a glow.

So here we frolic in the chill,
With laughter echoing, what a thrill!
In shimmering wonder, joy we'll find,
In every giggle that leaves us blind.

Heartbeats in the Cold

In the frosty air, I feel my heart,
Pounding like drums, it's quite the art.
A chilly walk, a valiant quest,
To find a warm drink, oh what a test.

Each heartbeat's like a little cheer,
As I navigate this winter sphere.
With mittens on and nose so red,
I stumble home, dreaming of bread.

The snowflakes fall, they tickle my face,
In this frozen world, I find my place.
With every heartbeat, I laugh and play,
In the cold embrace, I'll find my way.

So wrap me up in winters' bliss,
This chilly love, I can't dismiss.
For even in cold, my heart can sing,
With joy that only winter brings.

Hushed Gatherings

In the corner, cats do plot,
Whiskers twitch, a secret spot.
Sipping tea from tiny cups,
Trying not to wake the pups.

Conversations full of squeaks,
As the clock loudly creaks.
Mysteries of the mouse brigade,
Only heard when snacks are laid.

Under the table, a dog will snooze,
Dreaming of victory from last night's ruse.
Paws in the air, tail on the ground,
In this hush, peace is found.

Laughter floats on the chilly breeze,
As we play games with utmost ease.
The cat claims victory, yet again,
While the dog just sighs, "When will this end?"

Tinsel-Soft Evenings

Tinsel sparkles on the tree,
Cats think it's yarn; oh, woe is me!
Dogs jump in with festive cheer,
Oops, the ornaments disappear!

Hot cocoa spills on grandma's lap,
She laughs and says, "What a trap!"
Marshmallows fly like little snow,
Next thing you know, it's a cocoa show!

Twinkling lights flicker and fade,
The cat performs her grand charade.
With every jump and funny strut,
She leaves us all in giggles and gut!

As the evening settles in,
We toast to chaos, let the fun begin!
Who knew a night could be this wild?
With pets and laughter, we're all beguiled!

Frosty Touches

Morning frost on puppy's nose,
He sniffs the air; off he goes!
Chasing leaves, a wild ballet,
In winter's grasp, he wants to play.

Snowflakes tumble, soft and bright,
Cats in sweaters? What a sight!
They lounge in styles oh-so-chic,
While dogs are out, having a streak.

Hot cider warms up chilly hands,
We laugh at our frost-bit plans.
"More marshmallows!" we loudly cheer,
As we toast to winter's cheer!

But with the cold, comes silly slips,
Down we go, in frosty flips!
Yet, amid the shivers and the fun,
Our laughter sparkles like the sun!

Bright Hearts

Hearts are bright on this fine day,
Cats and dogs in the sun's warm ray.
Chasing tails and fun-filled plays,
Oh, how they brighten up our ways!

With wagging tails and purring sounds,
Joyful chaos that abounds.
Roll in grass, or chase a bee,
In this moment, we feel so free.

Snack time calls, oh what a scene,
Puppies look up, "Where's my cuisine?"
While kitties plot with calculating eyes,
Waiting for snacks, oh what a prize!

Evenings spark with glowing cheer,
With every bark, and every sneer.
Friends, both furry and dear to heart,
In a world of laughter, we'll never part.

Wonders of the Stillness

In stillness lies a curious sight,
A dog perplexed by the moonlight.
What barks back? He gives a stare,
His head tilts; it's just night air.

The cat, however, sits enthroned,
Proud as pie, she's well known.
Silent whiskers, a stealthy crouch,
She waits for whimsy, like a grouch.

Stars twinkle in the velvet sky,
While crickets chirp, a lullaby.
The world pauses; can you hear?
In wonder's stillness, there's no fear.

Nature whispers tales untold,
Furry friends, both brave and bold.
Together we dream, under starlit spree,
In stillness, we find our glee!

The Calm Before the Warmth

In January's frosty grip,
I dream of ice cream and a dip.
But snowflakes fall, a dance so bright,
I'll sip hot cocoa, it feels just right.

The sun hides behind a fluffy cloud,
While squirrels prance, their cheeks so proud.
"Hey, Mr. Penguin, take a seat,"
said the snowman with chill on his feet.

A warm day's coming, I just know,
But now I'm lost in this winter show.
So let's embrace the icy breeze,
And wear our mittens with so much ease.

With puffy jackets like marshmallows,
We'll chase each other like silly fellows.
The warm will come; soon we'll sweat,
But let's have fun, not a single regret.

Tucked Beneath Starry Chill

Under blankets, tucked away tight,
While outside, it's a chilling night.
The stars are winking, playing games,
But here inside, we're warm, not lame.

Frosted windows, the world so bright,
Hot chocolate streams, such a delight!
We giggle at the snowflakes' fall,
Tell tales of penguins, and snowballs.

The moon pops out, but we just snore,
Dreaming of summers and ice cream galore.
The chilly air makes us feel bold,
While wrapped in stories, bright and old.

Tomorrow's plans are quite a thrill,
But for now, we cozy and chill.
The winter's frosty, but that's alright,
For laughter shines in the starry night.

Frosted Laughter Underneath the Boughs

Underneath the frosty trees,
Snowflakes tumble with grace and ease.
We build a fort, it's quite a sight,
With laughter echoing; pure delight.

A snowball flies, oh what a throw!
Right at my buddy, now watch him glow.
He slips and slides, falls down, oh dear,
Now he's a snowman—eyes full of cheer!

The branches bow, as if they know,
Of secrets shared in the soft white glow.
With rosy cheeks and hearts so light,
Underneath boughs, we feel just right.

Laughter rings out like sleigh bells near,
Let's toast with cocoa, winter cheer!
We'll dance and sing till the sun breaks through,
Frosted laughter, forever true.

Echoes of Delight in the White Stillness

In the stillness of a winter's eve,
We hear the whispers of joy believe.
The crunch of snow beneath our feet,
Echoes of laughter; life is sweet.

Snowmen stand with a carrot nose,
Waving at us as we strike a pose.
With mittens flapping like big balloon,
We dance around, humming to the moon.

The cold holds no grip on our fun,
We'll skate on ponds, we'll run and run.
With frosty cheeks and smiles wide,
In this white stillness, we take our stride.

When spring arrives with a gentle sigh,
We'll reminisce 'neath the winter sky.
But now, let's frolic, let's embrace the night,
With echoes of delight, everything feels right.

Serene Flakes

Snowflakes dance in the air,
Landing gently in my hair.
I catch one upon my tongue,
Then laugh because I'm still so young.

Winter's got me feeling bold,
Building snowmen, joy untold.
A carrot nose and crooked grin,
I take a selfie, let the fun begin!

Sipping cocoa, marshmallows galore,
Chasing friends in a snowy war.
Laughter echoes, spirits high,
A winter wonderland, oh my!

But when it melts, oh what a fuss,
Where'd it go? I miss that bus!
The sun comes out, the snowflakes flee,
Just wait till next year, you'll see me!

Joyous Souls

In the chill of winter's night,
We gather round, everything feels right.
With snowball fights and games galore,
We're joyous souls, how could we ask for more?

Hot chocolate flows like rivers wide,
With marshmallows floating like a snow-white tide.
We share our stories, laughs so loud,
In this cozy moment, we feel so proud!

Snowflakes whirl, like dancers free,
Spinning joyfully, just like we.
A warm embrace, a friend's warm grin,
Who needs the sun when fun's within?

As snowflakes fall, we stomp and cheer,
Our hearts are light, filled with good cheer.
With joyous souls, we roam the night,
In winter's glow, we feel so right!

Frost-kissed Moments of Bliss

Frost-kissed mornings, what a sight,
Nature's artwork, pure delight.
Each breath a cloud, the air so clear,
Moments of bliss, oh winter dear!

Sledding down hills, we fly so fast,
Yelling and laughing, forgetting the past.
A tumble, a giggle, a little bit of pain,
We climb back up for another go again!

Card games by the fire's warm glow,
With playful banter, the fun will flow.
Nights filled with stories from winters' past,
In this cozy circle, we hope it will last.

When morning comes, the sun will rise,
But frost-kissed moments, they're the prize.
We carry them close, in our hearts so light,
Until the next snow, our spirits bright!

The Crystalline Lullaby

Whispers of winter, soft and low,
A crystalline lullaby begins to flow.
Snowflakes twinkle like stars in the night,
Hushing the world, making everything right.

The trees wear coats of sparkling white,
While children's laughter fills the night.
A snowman stands, proud and tall,
With a scarf so bright, he's loved by all!

The moon basks down with a silvery glow,
Mapping the paths where the soft winds blow.
We snuggle in blankets, warm and snug,
While hot cocoa hugs us, a tasty mug!

In crystalline dreams, we dance and play,
Our winter wonderland refuses to sway.
As lullabies whisper, our eyelids grow light,
Here's to dreams wrapped in frosty delight!

Embraced by the Winter's Glow

Embraced by the winter's golden glow,
We bundle up tight, and off we go.
Through frosty fields, we march with pride,
Making snow angels, side by side.

The chilly breeze plays with our hair,
While laughter echoes everywhere.
In this magic moment, we share the bliss,
A winter hug, a frozen kiss!

Hot soup awaits when the day is done,
A feast to celebrate all the fun.
With bellies full, we gather 'round,
Telling tales of joy we found.

As snowflakes fall, they whisper sweet,
In this winter glow, here's where we meet.
Together forever, through highs and lows,
Embraced by love in winter's glow!

Milton Keynes UK
Ingram Content Group UK Ltd.
UKHW022102091224
452221UK00007B/86